A Year to Remember - 1968
For Those Whose Hearts Belong to 1968

Celebrating your year
1968
A memorable year for

Content

Chapter 6: Technological Advancements and Popular Cars

Chapter 7: Stats and the Cost of Things

Chapter 8: Notable Births in 1968

Introduction

A Year to Remember - 1968
For Those Whose Hearts Belong to 1968

To our cherished readers who hold a special connection to the year 1968, whether it's because you were born in this remarkable year, celebrated a milestone, or hold dear memories from that time, this book is a tribute to you and your unique connection to an unforgettable era.

In the pages that follow, we invite you to embark on a captivating journey back to 1968, a year of profound historical significance. For those with a personal connection to this year, it holds a treasure trove of memories, stories, and experiences that shaped the world and touched your lives.

Throughout this book, we've woven together the tapestry of 1968, providing historical insights, personal stories, and interactive activities that allow you to relive and celebrate the significance of this special year.

As you turn the pages and immerse yourself in the events and culture of 1968, we hope you'll find moments of nostalgia, inspiration, and the opportunity to rekindle cherished memories of this extraordinary year.

This book is dedicated to you, our readers, who share a unique bond with 1968. May it bring you joy, enlightenment, and a deeper connection to the rich tapestry of history that weaves through your lives.

With warm regards,
Edward Art Lab

Chapter 1:
Politics and Leading Events around the World

1.1 The Global Stage in 1968: Where Were You?

Step into the transformative year of 1968, marked by global upheavals and cultural milestones. From the Prague Spring to space exploration, anti-war protests to iconic albums, this chapter delves into the pivotal events that shaped a tumultuous era.

Prague Spring: The Soviet Union invades Czechoslovakia and arrests President Dubcek

In a brutal suppression of political reforms, the Soviet Union invaded Czechoslovakia, crushing the Prague Spring movement. President Alexander Dubcek, a key figure in the push for liberalization, was arrested, marking a dark turn in Eastern European politics.

Assassination of Martin Luther King Jr. Leader of Negro Civil Rights Movement

The world mourned the loss of civil rights icon Martin Luther King Jr., who was assassinated in Memphis, Tennessee. King's leadership in the fight against racial injustice left an indelible mark on the struggle for equality and justice.

U.S. Senator Robert F. Kennedy's Assassination

Just months after Martin Luther King Jr.'s death, the United States was again shaken by tragedy when Senator Robert F. Kennedy, a charismatic political figure and advocate for civil rights, was assassinated in Los Angeles. His death marked another blow to a nation grappling with social and political upheaval.

Anti-Vietnam War Demonstrations in London Turn Violent

Amidst the global wave of protests against the Vietnam War, demonstrations in London turned violent in March. The anti-war movement, fueled by opposition to U.S. involvement in Vietnam, became a powerful force shaping political discourse.

NASA's Apollo 8 space mission was launched on December 21st.

A historic moment in space exploration occurred as NASA launched the Apollo 8 mission. This mission, orbiting the moon, marked significant progress in the race to land humans on the lunar surface.

General Strike in France: 800,000 March in Paris

France witnessed a massive one-day general strike as 800,000 teachers, workers, and students marched through Paris. The protest reflected widespread discontent and a desire for political and social change.

Tet Offensive: North Vietnam and Viet Cong Launch Attacks

The Vietnam War took a dramatic turn as North Vietnamese and Viet Cong forces launched the Tet Offensive. This large-scale surprise attack during the lunar new year led to intense fighting and had a profound impact on public perception of the war.

Dutch Elm Disease Continues to Ravage Trees

The destructive Dutch Elm Disease continued its spread, causing the destruction of tens of thousands of elm trees across affected regions. The epidemic had significant ecological and environmental consequences.

Creation of Redwood National Park in California

In a positive environmental development, the Redwood National Park was established in California to protect the iconic Giant Redwoods. This marked a commitment to preserving natural wonders for future generations.

The Beatles Release the "White Album"

Musical history was made as The Beatles released their self-titled double album, commonly known as the "White Album." The eclectic collection of songs showcased the band's versatility but received mixed reviews from critics.

Soviet Union - Zond 5 Space Mission

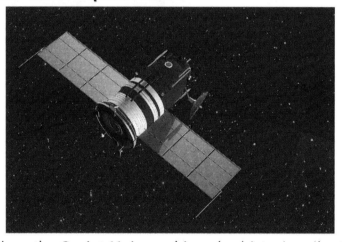

In September, the Soviet Union achieved a historic milestone with the Zond 5 space mission, marking the first successful orbit around the Moon and return to Earth. Carrying life forms like wine flies, mealworms, plants, bacteria, and tortoises, it became the inaugural mission to transport life to the Moon and bring it back. This accomplishment preceded the United States' Apollo 8 mission, where astronauts Frank Borman, James Lovell, and William Anders became the first humans to orbit and return from the Moon later that year.

US Presidential Conventions

- US political parties hold their conventions to formally choose presidential candidates during August.
- The Democratic National Convention is marked by violence as rioting erupts live on television after police are given orders by Chicago Mayor Daley to forcefully disperse peaceful anti-Vietnam war protesters.
- During the convention, Democrats had limited options as President Lyndon B. Johnson decided not to run and candidate Robert F. Kennedy was assassinated in June.
- They chose sitting Vice President Hubert Humphrey as the Presidential nominee and Senator Edmund S. Muskie for Vice President.
- In a more muted affair, the Republican National Convention was held in Miami Beach.
- The Republican delegates chose Richard M. Nixon, former Vice President under Eisenhower, as the presidential nominee and Spiro T. Agnew, Governor of Maryland, as the Vice Presidential nominee.

British Post office introduces First Class Post

In a shift in postal services, the British Post Office introduced First Class Post, offering a faster and premium mail delivery option for the first time.

China celebrates 20 years of communist rule by Mao Tse-tung

China marked two decades of communist rule under the leadership of Mao Tse-tung. The celebration reflected the enduring influence of the Communist Party in shaping the nation's political landscape.

RMS Queen Elizabeth - retired from service

The RMS Queen Elizabeth, once a majestic ocean liner, was retired from service, marking the end of an era in maritime history.

1.2 Leaders and Statesmen: Movers and Shakers of '68

Step into the world of 1968, where global leaders such as Dwight D. Eisenhower, Harold Macmillan, Sir Robert Menzies, and Nobusuke Kishi made indelible marks. Discover their significant roles, challenges, and contributions that shaped their nations and the global landscape during this transformative year.

United States - President Lyndon B. Johnson

Lyndon B. Johnson, often known as LBJ, served as the 36th President of the United States. He inherited the presidency after the assassination of John F. Kennedy in 1963. Johnson played a crucial role in the civil rights movement and the "Great Society" programs, focusing on social reforms.

United Kingdom -
Prime Minister Harold Wilson

Harold Wilson was the Prime Minister of the United Kingdom, serving two non-consecutive terms. His leadership during the late 1960s included addressing economic challenges and overseeing social reforms. Wilson's government implemented policies like the Open University and the abolition of the death penalty.

Canada - Prime Minister
Pierre Trudeau

Pierre Trudeau, a charismatic figure, became the 15th Prime Minister of Canada. Known for his progressive policies and commitment to bilingualism, Trudeau focused on social justice and individual freedoms. His leadership left a lasting impact on Canadian politics.

France - President Charles de Gaulle

Charles de Gaulle, a towering figure in French history, served as the President of France. A key player in World War II, he later led France through a period of post-war recovery. De Gaulle's leadership style and vision significantly influenced the nation's politics.

Germany -
Chancellor Kurt Georg Kiesinger

Kurt Georg Kiesinger held the position of Chancellor of West Germany. His chancellorship coincided with a time of social and political change in Germany. Kiesinger faced challenges related to student protests and the evolving dynamics of post-war Germany.

Italy -
Prime Minister Giovanni Leone

Giovanni Leone served as the Prime Minister of Italy. His tenure involved navigating the complex political landscape of Italian politics. Leone's leadership contributed to Italy's engagement with the European Economic Community (EEC).

René China -
Chairman of the People's Republic of China Liu Shaoqi

Liu Shaoqi played a significant role in the early years of the People's Republic of China. As Chairman, he focused on economic development but later fell out of favor during the Cultural Revolution under Mao Zedong's leadership.

Mexico - President Gustavo Diaz Ordaz

Gustavo Diaz Ordaz served as the President of Mexico during a period marked by social and political unrest. His presidency included the 1968 Mexico City Olympics and the Tlatelolco massacre, events that had a profound impact on Mexican history

Russia/Soviet Union - First Secretary of the CPSU Leonid Brezhnev

Leonid Brezhnev was a key figure in the leadership of the Soviet Union. As the First Secretary of the Communist Party, he presided over a period known as the "Era of Stagnation." His leadership style and policies shaped the Soviet Union during the late 1960s.

Activity: Historical Trivia Quiz
Test Your Knowledge of '68

1. Political Upheaval:
   - Which movement in Czechoslovakia was brutally suppressed by the Soviet Union in 1968?
     - a) Velvet Revolution
     - b) Prague Spring
     - c) Baltic Way
     - d) Iron Curtain

2. Civil Rights Loss:
   - Who was the influential civil rights leader assassinated in Memphis, Tennessee?
     - a) Malcolm X
     - b) Rosa Parks
     - c) Martin Luther King Jr.
     - d) John Lewis

3. Lunar Exploration:
   - What historic event in space exploration occurred on December 21st, 1968?
     - a) First Moon Landing
     - b) Mars Rover Launch
     - c) Apollo 8 Moon Orbit
     - d) Space Shuttle Maiden Voyage

4. French Protest Numbers:
   - How many teachers, workers, and students marched through Paris during the one-day general strike in France?
     - a) 500,000
     - b) 800,000
     - c) 1 million
     - d) 1.5 million

5. Democratic Nominee:

- Who became the Democratic presidential nominee in 1968 after the conventions?
  - a) John F. Kennedy
  - b) Hubert Humphrey
  - c) Robert F. Kennedy
  - d) Lyndon B. Johnson

6. British Postal Upgrade:

- What new mail delivery option was introduced by the British Post Office in 1968?
  - a) Express Mail
  - b) Priority Mail
  - c) First Class Post
  - d) Airmail Plus

7. Ocean Liner Retirement:

- Which majestic ocean liner was retired from service in 1968?
  - a) Titanic
  - b) RMS Queen Elizabeth
  - c) SS United States
  - d) Queen Mary

8. German Chancellor Challenges:

- Who faced challenges related to student protests as the Chancellor of West Germany?
  - a) Helmut Kohl
  - b) Willy Brandt
  - c) Kurt Georg Kiesinger
  - d) Konrad Adenauer

9. Mexican President's Term:
- Who was the President of Mexico during the 1968 Mexico City Olympics and the Tlatelolco massacre?
  - a) Vicente Fox
  - b) Adolfo López Mateos
  - c) Gustavo Diaz Ordaz
  - d) Felipe Calderón

10. Soviet Lunar Achievement:
- Which unmanned spacecraft achieved the first successful orbit around the Moon and return to Earth in 1968?
  - a) Luna 2
  - b) Vostok 1
  - c) Zond 5
  - d) Soyuz 4

Chapter 2:
The Iconic Movies, TV Shows, and Awards

2.1 Memorable Films of '68

Explore the cinematic wonders of 1968, from the action-packed "Bullitt" to the cultural resonance of "Night of the Living Dead," as we delve into the memorable films that left an indelible mark on the year.

Bullitt

"Bullitt" roared onto the screen as a classic action thriller, featuring Steve McQueen in a memorable car chase through the streets of San Francisco. The film set new standards for its realistic portrayal of police work and earned acclaim for its gripping narrative.

Oliver

The musical drama "Oliver" brought Charles Dickens' timeless tale to life, with memorable performances and catchy tunes. The film received critical acclaim, including multiple Academy Awards, and remains a beloved classic.

Chitty Chitty Bang Bang

"Chitty Chitty Bang Bang" enchanted audiences with its whimsical tale of a magical car and its adventures. Filled with fantastical elements and musical delights, the film captivated viewers of all ages.

Night of the Living Dead

George A. Romero's "Night of the Living Dead" revolutionized the horror genre, introducing the concept of zombies as we know them today. The film's social commentary and chilling atmosphere left a lasting impact on the world of cinema.

The Graduate

"The Graduate" emerged as a cultural phenomenon, exploring themes of love and disillusionment in the midst of societal changes. Dustin Hoffman's portrayal of Benjamin Braddock became iconic, and the film's soundtrack, featuring Simon & Garfunkel, added to its timeless appeal.

Guess Who's Coming to Dinner

This groundbreaking film addressed racial and societal issues in a thought-provoking manner. "Guess Who's Coming to Dinner" starred Sidney Poitier and tackled interracial relationships, earning acclaim for its powerful performances and relevant themes.

Bonnie and Clyde

"Bonnie and Clyde" revolutionized the portrayal of violence in cinema and marked a shift in Hollywood storytelling. The film's bold narrative, stylish direction, and stellar performances by Warren Beatty and Faye Dunaway left an indelible mark.

The Odd Couple

Neil Simon's classic comedy "The Odd Couple" transitioned from the stage to the big screen, showcasing the comedic genius of Jack Lemmon and Walter Matthau. The film's portrayal of mismatched roommates became a template for future buddy comedies.

Planet of the Apes

"Planet of the Apes" transported audiences to a dystopian future where apes ruled and humans were enslaved. The film's iconic twist ending and its exploration of societal themes made it a landmark in science fiction cinema.

Rosemary's Baby

Directed by Roman Polanski, "Rosemary's Baby" immersed audiences in psychological horror. Mia Farrow's gripping performance and the film's atmosphere of suspense contributed to its status as a classic in the horror genre.

2.2 TV Shows That Captivated the Nation

Embark on a journey through the television landscape of 1968 as we explore the shows that captivated the nation, from the groundbreaking humor of "Rowan and Martin's Laugh-In" to the iconic Western saga "Bonanza" and the beloved military comedy "Gomer Pyle, U.S.M.C."

Rowan and Martin's Laugh-in

A revolutionary sketch comedy show, "Laugh-In" embraced irreverence and rapid-fire humor. Hosted by Dan Rowan and Dick Martin, it featured a mix of zany sketches, memorable catchphrases, and an ensemble cast that included Goldie Hawn and Lily Tomlin.

60 minutes

Debuting as a groundbreaking news magazine, "60 Minutes" set the standard for investigative journalism. With its iconic ticking stopwatch, the show, anchored by Mike Wallace and others, delved into in-depth reporting, interviews, and features that covered a spectrum of topics.

Gomer Pyle, U.S.M.C.

A spin-off from "The Andy Griffith Show," "Gomer Pyle, U.S.M.C." followed the misadventures of the lovable and naive Gomer Pyle, played by Jim Nabors, as he navigates life in the Marine Corps. The show provided a comedic take on military life and resonated with audiences.

Mayberry R.F.D

A spin-off of "The Andy Griffith Show," "Mayberry R.F.D." continued the small-town charm of Mayberry. Centered around the character of Sam Jones, played by Ken Berry, the show maintained the wholesome humor and community spirit of its predecessor.

Hawaii Five 0

A classic police procedural drama, "Hawaii Five-O" followed the investigations of the fictional Hawaii State Police. Led by the tough and charismatic Steve McGarrett, played by Jack Lord, the show combined crime-solving with the allure of the Hawaiian setting.

The Doris Day Show

A sitcom starring the legendary Doris Day, the show depicted her character's life as a widowed mother living on a farm with her two sons. With Day's charm and humor, the series offered a lighthearted take on family dynamics and rural living.

Bonanza

As one of the longest-running Western series, "Bonanza" chronicled the lives of the Cartwright family on the Ponderosa Ranch. With patriarch Ben Cartwright and his three sons, the show explored themes of family, morality, and the challenges of the Old West.

2.3 Prestigious Film Awards and Honors

In the glittering realm of 1968 cinema, accolades and honors shone bright. Let's delve into the prestigious awards that celebrated outstanding performances and cinematic excellence during this golden era.

40th Academy Awards (Oscars):

- Best Picture: "In the Heat of the Night"
- Best Director: Mike Nichols for "The Graduate"
- Best Actor: Rod Steiger for "In the Heat of the Night"
- Best Actress: Katharine Hepburn for "Guess Who's Coming to Dinner"
- Best Supporting Actor: George Kennedy for "Cool Hand Luke"
- Best Supporting Actress: Estelle Parsons for "Bonnie and Clyde"
- Best Story and Screenplay Written Directly for the Screen: "Guess Who's Coming to Dinner" – William Rose
- Best Screenplay Based on Material from Another Medium: "In the Heat of the Night" – Stirling Silliphant based on the novel by John Ball

25th Golden Globe Awards:

- Best Motion Picture - Drama: "In the Heat of the Night"
- Best Motion Picture - Comedy or Musical: "The Graduate"
- Best Actor - Drama: Rod Steiger - In the Heat of the Night as Police Chief Bill Gillespie
- Best Actress - Drama: Edith Evans - The Whisperers as Maggie Ross
- Best Director: Mike Nichols - The Graduate
- Best Screenplay: In the Heat of the Night - Stirling Silliphant

21th British Academy Film Awards:

- Best Film: "A Man for All Seasons"
- Best British Film: "A Man for All Seasons"
- Best Foreign Actor: Rod Steiger – In the Heat of the Night as Chief Bill Gillespie
- Best British Actor: Paul Scofield – A Man for All Seasons as Thomas More
- Best British Actress: Edith Evans – The Whisperers as Mrs. Ross
- Best Foreign Actress: Anouk Aimée – A Man and a Woman as Anne Gauthier
- Best British Screenplay: "A Man for All Seasons" – Robert Bolt
- Best Animated Film: Notes on a Triangle – René Jodoin

Activity:

Movie Trivia Quiz
How Well Do You Know '68 Entertainment?

Step back in time to the cinematic and television wonders of 1968 with our engaging crossword quiz! This activity will test your knowledge of the iconic movies and TV shows that captivated audiences during this transformative year in entertainment.

ACROSS

1. The iconic action thriller featuring Steve McQueen and a memorable car chase through San Francisco.

3. Neil Simon's classic comedy showcasing the comedic genius of Jack Lemmon and Walter Matthau.

4. Classic police procedural drama set in Hawaii, led by tough and charismatic Steve McGarrett.

5. Groundbreaking news magazine that set the standard for investigative journalism with its iconic ticking stopwatch.

7. Charles Dickens' timeless tale brought to life in a musical drama that received critical acclaim.

DOWN

2. The cultural phenomenon exploring themes of love and disillusionment, starring Dustin Hoffman.

6. Classic Western series chronicling the lives of the Cartwright family on the Ponderosa Ranch.

Chapter 3:
Music: Top Songs and Albums

3.1 Chart-Toppers

Delve into the musical landscape of 1968, where these tunes dominated the charts and became timeless classics.

Hey Jude - The Beatles

Released as a single in August 1968, "Hey Jude" by The Beatles, with its extended length and unconventional structure, became a groundbreaking song. Written by Paul McCartney for John Lennon's son, Julian, the song spent nine weeks at the top of the charts. Its emotional depth, memorable melody, and the famous coda featuring the repeated "na-na-na" made it an enduring classic.

Love is Blue - Paul Mauriat

In 1968, Paul Mauriat's "Love is Blue" became an instrumental sensation. Originally composed by André Popp, the song's lush orchestration, particularly the distinctive sound of the lead electric guitar, contributed to its success. The soothing yet melancholic tune earned Mauriat a Grammy Award and held the number one spot on the charts.

Honey - Bobby Goldsboro

Bobby Goldsboro's "Honey" touched hearts with its poignant narrative. Released in 1968, the song tells the story of love, loss, and heartbreak. Goldsboro's emotive delivery and the tragic tale resonated with audiences, making it a chart-topping ballad.

(Sittin' On) The Dock of the Bay - Otis Redding

Otis Redding's "(Sittin' On) The Dock of the Bay" showcased a different side of the legendary soul singer. Released posthumously in 1968, the song blended soul with a touch of folk. Its distinctive whistling and Redding's raw, introspective lyrics contributed to its success, making it one of his most iconic songs.

People Got to Be Free - The Rascals

The Rascals' "People Got to Be Free" delivered a powerful message of unity and hope during a turbulent era. Released in 1968, the song became an anthem for the civil rights and peace movements. Its upbeat, soulful sound and socially conscious lyrics propelled it to the top of the charts.

Those Were the Days - Marry Hopkin

Mary Hopkin's "Those Were the Days," produced by Paul McCartney, became a folk-pop sensation in 1968. The song, with its nostalgic lyrics and Hopkin's melodic vocals, captured the essence of looking back on simpler times. It quickly climbed the charts and established Hopkin as a notable artist.

What a Wonderful World - Louis Armstrong

Louis Armstrong's "What a Wonderful World" remains a timeless classic. Released in 1968, the song's optimistic lyrics and Armstrong's signature gravelly voice created a beautiful ode to the joys of life. Despite initial modest chart success, it has since become one of Armstrong's most celebrated and enduring recordings.

3.2 Music Awards and Honors

10th Annual Grammy Awards

- **Record of the Year:** "Up, Up and Away," 5th Dimension
- **Album of the Year:** Sgt. Pepper's Lonely Hearts Club Band, The Beatles (Capitol)
- **Song of the Year:** "Up, Up and Away," Jimmy L. Webb, songwriter
- **Best New Artist:** Bobbie Gentry
- **Best Vocal Performance, Male:** "By the Time I Get to Phoenix," Glen Campbell
- **Best Vocal Performance, Female:** "Ode to Billie Joe," Bobbie Gentry
- **Best Performance By a Vocal Group (Two to Six Persons):** "Up, Up and Away," 5th Dimension
- **Best Contemporary Single:** "Up, Up and Away," 5th Dimension
- **Best Contemporary Album:** Sgt. Pepper's Lonely Hearts Club Band, The Beatles (Capitol)
- **Best Contemporary Male Solo Vocal Performance:** "By the Time I Get to Phoenix," Glen Campbell
- **Best Contemporary Female Solo Vocal Performance:** "Ode to Billie Joe," Bobbie Gentry
- **Best Contemporary Group Performance, Vocal or Instrumental:** "Up, Up and Away," 5th Dimension
- **Best Rhythm and Blues Recording:** "Respect," Aretha Franklin (Atlantic)
- **Best Rhythm and Blues Solo Vocal Performance, Male:** "Dead End Street," Lou Rawls
- **Best Rhythm and Blues Solo Vocal Performance, Female:** "Respect," Aretha Franklin
- **Best Rhythm and Blues Group Performance, Vocal or Instrumental (Two or More):** "Soul Man," Sam and Dave

Activity: Music Lyrics Challenge - Guess the Song Lyrics from '68

Instructions:

1. Read the provided information about the top songs and albums from 1968.
2. Based on the details given, try to identify the song lyrics associated with each mentioned track.
3. Write down your guesses on a piece of paper.
4. After making your guesses, compare them with the correct answers provided below.

Song Lyrics:

1. "Remember to let her into your heart, then you can start to make it better."
2. "Sitting on the dock of the bay, watching the tide roll away. Ooo, I'm just sittin' on the dock of the bay, wastin' time."
3. "Look at the stars, look how they shine for you, and everything you do. Yeah, they were all yellow."
4. "What a wonderful world. I see trees of green, red roses too. I see them bloom for me and you."
5. "Honey, I miss you, and I'm being good. And I'd love to be with you, if only I could."
6. "Once upon a time, there was a tavern, where we used to raise a glass or two. Remember how we laughed away the hours."
7. "Love is blue, blue is the color of our love. Blue are the feelings that live inside me."

Scoring:

- 6-7 correct: Music Maestro! You nailed it.
- 4-5 correct: Impressive! You have a good knowledge of '68 lyrics.
- 2-3 correct: Not bad! You're on the right track.
- 1 correct: Keep listening to those classic tunes and give it another shot!

Chapter 4:Sports in 1968:
A Journey Through the World of Athletics

4.1 Athletic Achievements and Memorable Victories

Australian Tennis Open

- Jan 29 Australian Championships Men's Tennis: Australian Bill Bowrey wins his first and only Grand Slam title; beats Juan Gisbert Sr. of Spain 7-5, 2-6, 9-7, 6-4

Tennis Player
Bill Bowrey

- Jan 29 Australian Championships Women's Tennis: American Billie Jean King beats home favourite Margaret Court 6-1, 6-2 for her 13th Grand Slam singles title

Tennis Player
Billie Jean King

Winter Olympics

Feb 6 X Winter Olympic Games opens in Grenoble, France

These are the top ten nations that won medals at the 1968 Winter Games.

Rank	Nation	Gold	Silver	Bronze	Total
1	Norway	6	6	2	14
2	Soviet Union	5	5	3	13
3	France	4	3	2	9
4	Italy	4	0	0	4
5	Austria	3	4	4	11
6	Netherlands	3	3	3	9
7	Sweden	3	2	3	8
8	West Germany	2	2	3	7
9	United States	1	5	1	7
10	East Germany	1	2	2	5
10	Finland	1	2	2	5
Total (10 entries)		**33**	**34**	**25**	**92**

Feb 18 X Winter Olympic Games close in Grenoble, France

Summer Olympics

Oct 12 IXX Summer Olympic Games open at Mexico City, Mexico; first Olympics in Latin America

These are the top ten nations that won medals at the 1968 Games. Host Mexico won 9 medals in total.

Rank	Nation	Gold	Silver	Bronze	Total
1	United States	45	28	34	107
2	Soviet Union	29	32	30	91
3	Japan	11	7	7	25
4	Hungary	10	10	12	32
5	East Germany	9	9	7	25
6	France	7	3	5	15
7	Czechoslovakia	7	2	4	13
8	West Germany	5	11	10	26
9	Australia	5	7	5	17
10	Great Britain	5	5	3	13
Total (10 entries)		**133**	**114**	**117**	**364**

Grand National (Mar 30)

The 122nd Grand National witnessed the rise of a young star. Brian Fletcher, a 20-year-old jockey, astride the 100/7 chance Red Alligator, embarked on a historic journey. This marked the first of his three Grand National victories, etching his name in the annals of horse racing lore.

Boxing Title Fight (Mar 4)

The Madison Square Garden in New York City bore witness to Joe Frazier's relentless pursuit of greatness. With a record standing at an impeccable 20-0, Frazier captured the vacant world heavyweight boxing title in a thrilling 11th round TKO against Buster Mathis. The boxing world had found a new champion, and Frazier's journey had only just begun.

European Cup Winner's Cup (May 23)

In Rotterdam, AC Milan of Italy secured their 8th European Cup Winner's Cup, triumphing over Hamburger SV of West Germany with a decisive 2-0 victory. The pitch echoed with the cheers of victory as AC Milan added another illustrious chapter to their storied football legacy.

European Cup (May 29)

Wembley Stadium in London set the stage for history as Manchester United, led by the legendary Bobby Charlton, emerged victorious in the European Cup Final. Charlton's two goals propelled the English club to a resounding 4-1 victory over Benfica, marking a historic moment as the first English club to clinch the coveted trophy.

UEFA European Championship (Jun 10)

The Stadio Olimpico in Rome bore witness to the UEFA European Championship Final, where Italy secured a 2-0 victory over Yugoslavia in a replay, following a 1-1 draw in the initial encounter. The echoes of triumph reverberated through the stadium as Italy claimed European football glory.

Ballon d'Or (Dec 24)

On Christmas Eve, the prestigious Ballon d'Or was bestowed upon George Best, the dynamic winger from Manchester United. Best's dazzling performances earned him the title of the best European football player, making him the first Northern Irish national to receive this esteemed accolade.

Boston Marathon (Apr 15)

The 72nd Boston Marathon witnessed historic moments as Amby Burfoot claimed victory with a time of 2:22:17. Notably, Bobbi Gibb made history as the first woman to participate for the third consecutive year, even in the absence of official sanctioning.

Indy 500 (May 30)

The roar of engines filled the air at the Indianapolis 500 as Bobby Unser, driving a piston-powered Offenhauser, triumphed over Dan Gurney. This marked the first of Unser's three Indy 500 victories, solidifying his place among the legends of American open-wheel racing.

Tour de France (Jul 21)

The 55th Tour de France unfolded with Jan Janssen of the Netherlands emerging as the champion. Janssen's cycling prowess and determination led him to victory in one of the most prestigious events in the world of cycling.

F1 World Champion (Nov 3)

The Formula 1 World Drivers Championship culminated in a thrilling race at the Autódromo Hermanos Rodríguez in Mexico. English Lotus driver Graham Hill secured his second title, winning the Mexican Grand Prix and finishing 12 points ahead of the formidable Scotsman, Jackie Stewart.

4.2 American Sports: Champions and Championship Moments
World Series (Oct 10)

The stage was set at Busch Memorial Stadium as the Detroit Tigers clashed with the St. Louis Cardinals in the Baseball World Series. In a series that echoed with anticipation, the Tigers emerged victorious, clinching a 4-3 win. The final triumph came on October 10 when Tigers pitcher Mickey Lolich dazzled, earning himself the MVP title and etching his name into the annals of baseball history.

Stanley Cup (May 11)

The Montreal Forum in Quebec witnessed a spectacle as the Montreal Canadiens faced off against the St. Louis Blues in the Stanley Cup Final. In a 4-0 series sweep, defenseman J. C. Tremblay fired home the winner, securing the coveted cup for the Canadiens and leaving an indelible mark on the rich history of ice hockey.

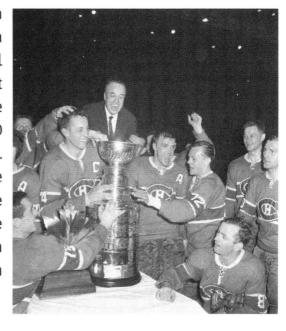

NBA All-Star Game (Jan 23)

Madison Square Garden in New York City hosted the 18th NBA All-Star Game, where the East triumphed over the West with a score of 144-124. Hal Greer of the Philadelphia 76ers showcased his skills, earning the MVP title and contributing to the East's victory in this star-studded basketball spectacle.

NBA Championship (May 2)

The 22nd NBA Championship saw the Boston Celtics facing off against the LA Lakers. In a gripping series that went six games, the Celtics emerged triumphant, securing the championship with a 4-2 series win. The courtside drama unfolded, adding another chapter to the storied rivalry between these basketball powerhouses.

NHL All-Star Game (Jan 16)

Maple Leaf Gardens hosted the 21st NHL All-Star Game, where the Toronto Maple Leafs clashed with the All-Stars. In a closely contested battle, the Maple Leafs emerged victorious with a 4-3 win, and goaltender Bruce Gamble earned the MVP title for his stellar performance, showcasing the prowess of Canadian ice hockey talent.

CFL Grey Cup (Nov 30)

The CNE Stadium in Toronto bore witness to the CFL Grey Cup, where the Ottawa Rough Riders clashed with the Calgary Stampeder. In a game filled with gridiron intensity, the Rough Riders emerged triumphant with a 24-21 victory. Vic Washington's 79-yard TD run became a Grey Cup record, etching his name into the lore of Canadian football.

Activity: Sports Trivia - Test Your Knowledge of 1968 Sports History

Instructions: Answer the following questions based on the information provided.

Questions:

1. Who won the Australian Championships Women's Tennis in 1968, defeating Margaret Court?
2. In the 122nd Grand National, who was the 20-year-old jockey riding the horse Red Alligator to victory?
3. Which Italian football club secured their 8th European Cup Winner's Cup in 1968, beating Hamburger SV in Rotterdam?
4. Who scored twice in the European Cup Final at Wembley Stadium, leading Manchester United to a 4-1 victory over Benfica?
5. Which cyclist emerged as the champion in the 55th Tour de France in 1968?
6. In the NBA Championship of 1968, which teams faced off, and who emerged as the winner?
7. Who was awarded the Ballon d'Or on December 24, 1968, becoming the first Northern Irish national to receive the award?
8. Which team won the Stanley Cup in 1968, and who scored the decisive goal in the final?
9. In the 22nd NBA Championship, how many games did the Boston Celtics take to defeat the LA Lakers?
10. Which horse won the 1968 Baseball World Series for the Detroit Tigers, and who was named the MVP?

Chapter 5: Pop Culture, Fashion, and Popular Leisure Activities

5.1 Fashion Flashback: What the World Wore in '68

Explore the sartorial choices that defined the fashion landscape of 1968, where elegance and rebellion converged in a tapestry of iconic styles.

Women's fashion:
Ethnic prints

Women embraced the global influence in their attire, adorning themselves with vibrant ethnic prints and bold floral patterns. Dresses and skirts became canvases for rich, diverse designs, reflecting a spirit of cultural exploration.

Colorful jewelry

Accessorizing took center stage with the introduction of colorful jewelry. Chunky beaded necklaces, large hoop earrings, and intricate bracelets became essential elements, adding a playful and eclectic touch to outfits.

High-wasted pants

Departing from the conventional, high-waisted pants became a defining trend. This style not only offered a deviation from traditional cuts but also contributed to the evolving narrative of women's fashion, symbolizing a break from established norms.

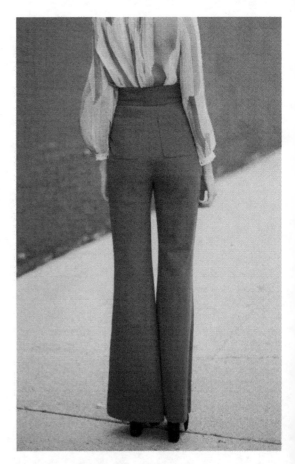

Long straight hairstyles

Hair took on a free-flowing and natural vibe with long, straight hairstyles. Often parted in the center, this look embodied the carefree and liberated spirit of the late '60s, aligning with the broader cultural shifts of the time.

Men's fashion:

Turtlenecks

Turtlenecks emerged as a staple in men's fashion, providing a sophisticated yet versatile option. Paired with various ensembles, from suits to casual wear, turtlenecks became synonymous with a sense of refinement and style.

Wide-legged pants

Departing from the slim cuts of previous years, wide-legged pants made a bold statement. This style, characterized by loose and flowing silhouettes, reflected the broader shift towards more relaxed and unconventional fashion choices.

Pinstriped suits

Men embraced pinstriped suits as a symbol of classic elegance. The subtle yet distinctive pattern added a touch of sophistication, making these suits suitable for both formal and semi-formal occasions.

Vests

Vests made a comeback, becoming a fashionable layering element in men's wardrobes. Worn over shirts or turtlenecks, vests added a touch of flair and individuality to outfits, reflecting the experimental nature of fashion in the late '60s.

Nehru jackets

Inspired by Indian fashion, Nehru jackets gained popularity. Featuring a distinctive mandarin collar, these jackets represented a fusion of global influences, showcasing the era's fascination with diverse cultural elements.

5.2. 1968 Slang

The slang of 1968 was a vibrant linguistic tapestry reflecting the countercultural spirit and social upheavals of the time. Here are some popular expressions that captured the essence of the era:

Gimme some skin = Shake hands

An informal way to say "shake hands," this expression embodied the camaraderie and connection shared among individuals, emphasizing a sense of unity.

Lay it on me = Tell me

A request for information, asking someone to share details or insights. This phrase reflected the open and communicative nature of the youth culture, where information exchange was valued.

Outta sight = Awesome

Used to describe something impressive or excellent, "outta sight" conveyed a sense of awe and admiration. It celebrated the extraordinary and the avant-garde, aligning with the experimental spirit of the late '60s.

Let's jam = Leaving a place

A colloquial way to express the act of leaving a place or departing. This informal phrase added a musical twist to everyday language, contributing to the infusion of music and lifestyle.

Hang loose = Relax

Encouraging others to relax and take it easy, "hang loose" embodied the laid-back attitude of the era. It encouraged individuals to go with the flow and not stress over the small stuff.

Going steady = Dating

A term indicating a committed dating relationship. While the concept of "going steady" had been around for a while, it continued to be part of the dating vernacular, reflecting the evolving dynamics of romantic relationships.

Activity:
Fashion Design Coloring Page - Create Your '68-Inspired Outfit

Share your 1968 photos,
Don't forget to show off your fabulous '68 fashion

Chapter 6: Technological Advancements and Popular Cars

6.1 Innovations That Shaped the Future

The year 1968 marked a period of groundbreaking technological advancements that propelled society into a new era. Here are some key innovations that left an indelible mark:

Boeing 747 Maiden Flight

The iconic Boeing 747, known as the "Queen of the Skies," took its maiden flight in 1968. This jumbo jet revolutionized air travel, offering unprecedented passenger capacity and shaping the future of aviation.

Air Bags

In a significant stride toward automotive safety, Allen K. Breed introduced the concept of air bags. These safety devices automatically deployed and inflated on violent impact, utilizing nitrogen gas to provide a cushioning barrier for vehicle occupants.

First Successful Heart Transplant

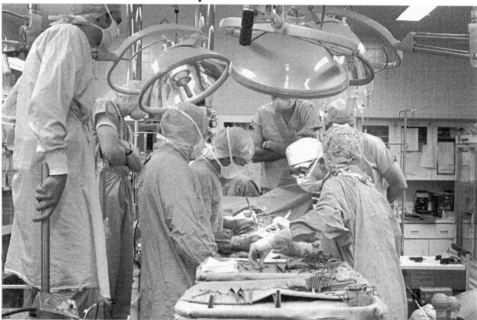

Dr. Christian Barnard achieved a medical milestone by conducting the world's first successful heart transplant. This groundbreaking procedure opened new frontiers in organ transplantation and medical possibilities.

US Experimental Hydrogen Bomb

The United States conducted tests on an experimental hydrogen bomb, underscoring the intense technological competition and geopolitical tensions of the Cold War era.

Emergency 911 Telephone Service

The introduction of the Emergency 911 Telephone Service in the USA marked a crucial development in public safety. This centralized emergency number provided a streamlined and efficient way for individuals to report emergencies, ensuring rapid response and assistance available 24/7.

ATM (Automated Teller Machine)

First Philadelphia Bank installed the inaugural Automated Teller Machine (ATM) in the U.S. This innovation transformed banking by allowing customers to conduct various transactions independently, paving the way for the modern banking experience.

6.2 The Automobiles of '68
Alfa Romeo 1750 Berlina

An elegant sedan by Alfa Romeo, the 1750 Berlina combined Italian flair with practicality, featuring a sleek design and robust performance.

AMC AMX

The American Motors Corporation (AMC) AMX stood out as a two-seater muscle car, emphasizing speed and agility. Its distinctive design and powerful engine made it a symbol of American performance.

Audi 100 Coupé S

Audi's 100 Coupé S exemplified German engineering with a sporty and stylish design. This compact coupe offered a balance of performance and sophistication.

BMW E9

The BMW E9 series represented the epitome of luxury sports cars. With its graceful lines and powerful engines, it solidified BMW's reputation for producing high-performance vehicles.

Ferrari Daytona

The Ferrari Daytona, officially known as the 365 GTB/4, was a mid-engine grand tourer, showcasing the iconic Ferrari styling and performance that enthusiasts cherished.

Ford Torino

Ford's Torino was a dynamic addition to the American muscle car scene. Its aggressive design and potent engines contributed to its popularity in the high-performance segment.

Ginetta G4

The Ginetta G4, a British sports car, embodied the spirit of lightweight racing machines. Its nimble handling and minimalist design attracted those seeking an authentic driving experience.

Holden Brougham

Holden's Brougham, an Australian luxury sedan, offered a spacious and comfortable ride. It catered to those desiring elegance and modern amenities.

Isuzu 117 Coupé

The Isuzu 117 Coupé, a Japanese innovation, combined sleek aesthetics with reliable performance, showcasing Isuzu's prowess in crafting stylish vehicles.

Jaguar XJ

Jaguar's XJ series represented British luxury at its finest. With its graceful design and refined features, it set a standard for premium sedans.

Lamborghini Espada

Lamborghini's Espada was a groundbreaking four-seat grand tourer, showcasing the brand's commitment to performance and luxury.

Mercedes-Benz W115

The Mercedes-Benz W115 series, known as the "Stroke Eight," embodied the brand's dedication to quality and innovation, offering a range of body styles to suit diverse preferences.

Nissan Laurel

Nissan's Laurel represented Japanese automotive sophistication, featuring a blend of style and practicality that appealed to a broad audience.

Activity: Car logo quiz
Guess the car logo

Introduction: In this quiz, you'll see images of car logos with a gap. Your task is to guess the car brand and complete the missing letters to correctly identify the logo. Good luck!

1. _____   2. _____

3. _____   4. _____

5. _____   6. _____

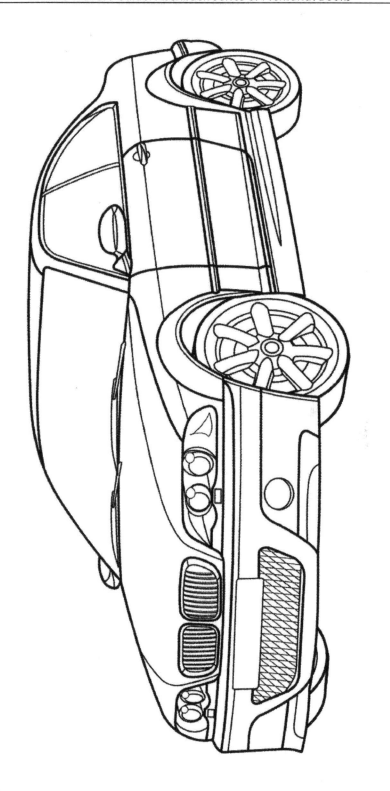

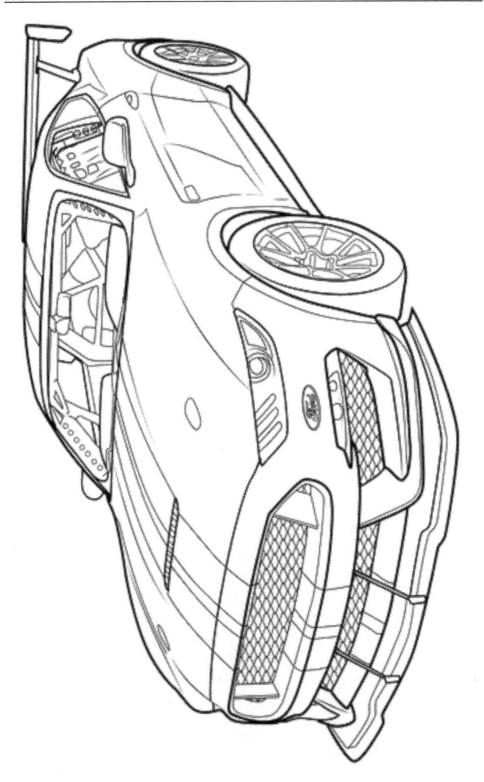

Chapter 7: Stats and the Cost of Things

7.1 The Price Tag: Cost of Living in 1968

In 1968, the cost of living was marked by a combination of post-war recovery and the emergence of new economic trends. Here's a glimpse into the price tags of various commodities and services:

- Average cost of New house $14,950.00

- Average Monthly Rent $130.00
- Average Income per year $7,850.00
- The Federal Hourly Minimum Wage is $1.60 an hour
- Gerbers baby Food 25 cents for 3

- Average Cost of a new car $2,750.00

- Cost of a gallon of Gas 34 cents

- Cost of a gallon of Milk $1.07

- Casual Living Room Set $229.95

- Dozen eggs 53 cents

- Movie Ticket $1.50

7.2 Dollars and Sense: Inflation and Its Effects

Yearly Inflation Rate USA 4.27%

In 1968, the United States experienced a notable yearly inflation rate of 4.27%. This figure indicates the percentage increase in the general price level of goods and services over the course of the year. While 4.27% falls within the moderate range of inflation, it signifies a period of economic activity with prices gradually on the rise. Factors such as increased demand, production costs, or external economic pressures may have contributed to this inflationary trend.

Understanding the inflation rate is crucial for assessing the purchasing power of currency and its impact on consumers, businesses, and the overall economy. Moderate inflation can stimulate spending and investment but may also lead to concerns about the erosion of real wages.

Year End Close Dow Jones 943

The Dow Jones Industrial Average, a prominent stock market index, concluded the year with a closing value of 943 points. The Dow Jones index reflects the aggregate performance of major publicly traded companies, serving as a barometer for the overall health of the stock market.

A year-end close of 943 suggests a robust performance in the stock market during 1968. Investors likely witnessed positive returns on their investments, and this figure represents the collective valuation of the included companies at the close of the trading year. It's important to note that stock market performance is influenced by various economic factors, including corporate earnings, interest rates, and geopolitical events.

Activity: 1968 Shopping List Challenge

Take this shopping journey through time, create a shopping list with these items, calculate the total cost, and consider how these prices compare to today's standards.

Shopping List:

- Average Cost of new house $14,950.00
- Cost of a gallon of Gas 34 cents
- Average Cost New Car $2,750.00
- Gallon of Milk $1.07
- Bacon per pound 65 cents
- Movie Ticket $1.50
- Dozen eggs 53 cents
- First-class Stamp $0.05
- Air conditioner, 5000 BTU, $99.00/each
- Washing machine, Hotpoint, $159.00/each
- Candles, Citronella, $1.00/3
- Soap, Dove, $0.37/2 regular bars
- Newspaper $0.10/daily paper
- Television, Panasonic, 88 square inch viewing area, $69.95/each
- Women's shoes, Naturalizer, $11.00-19.00/pair

Introduction:

1. Create a shopping list that includes all the items from the list above.
2. Next to each item, write down its 1968 price.
3. Calculate the total cost of your shopping list in 1968 prices.
4. Now, let's bring this challenge to the present. Research and find the approximate prices of these same items today.
5. Create a second column on your list and write down the modern prices for each item.

6. Calculate the total cost of your shopping list using today's prices.

7. Compare the total costs in 1968 and today. Calculate the percentage increase in prices over the years.

8. Reflect on how the cost of living has changed between 1968 and today. What factors do you think contributed to these price differences?

SHOPPING List 1968

	Item	Price	# Units	Total Price
☐				
☐				
☐				
☐				
☐				
☐				
☐				
☐				
☐				
☐				
☐				
☐				
☐				
☐				
☐				
☐				
☐				
☐				
☐				
☐				
			Total	

SHOPPING *List* Today

	Item	Price	# Units	Total Price
☐				
☐				
☐				
☐				
☐				
☐				
☐				
☐				
☐				
☐				
☐				
☐				
☐				
☐				
☐				
☐				
☐				
☐				
☐				
☐				
☐				
			Total	

This activity will give you a perspective on the value of money and how inflation has affected our purchasing power over time. Have fun with your 1968 Shopping List Challenge!

Chapter 8:Notable Births in 1968

The year 1968 witnessed the arrival of several individuals who would go on to shape the cultural, technological, and entertainment landscapes. Let's delve into the notable births of that year:

Will Smith (September 25t)

Born in Philadelphia, Will Smith rose to fame as a rapper in the duo DJ Jazzy Jeff & The Fresh Prince before transitioning to acting. His charismatic performances in "The Fresh Prince of Bel-Air" and blockbuster films like "Independence Day" and "Men in Black" solidified his status as a Hollywood icon.

Naomi Watts (September 28th)

Hailing from England, Naomi Watts gained acclaim for her versatile acting skills. Her breakthrough roles in films such as "Mulholland Drive" and "The Ring" showcased her ability to tackle diverse and challenging characters.

Jerry Yang (November 6th)

As a co-founder of Yahoo!, Jerry Yang played a pivotal role in the early days of the internet. His contributions to the development of one of the first widely used web portals marked a significant milestone in the digital era.

Celine Dion (March 30th)

Canadian powerhouse Celine Dion became a global sensation with her exceptional vocal range and emotional delivery. Her chart-topping hits, including "My Heart Will Go On" from the "Titanic" soundtrack, made her one of the best-selling female artists in the world.

Hugh Jackman (October 12th)

Hailing from Australia, Hugh Jackman's career is synonymous with versatility. Renowned for his portrayal of Wolverine in the "X-Men" franchise, Jackman seamlessly transitioned between theater, film, and television, earning critical acclaim for his diverse roles.

Daniel Craig (March 2nd)

English actor Daniel Craig is best known for his portrayal of James Bond, bringing a gritty and realistic dimension to the iconic spy character. His performances in films like "Casino Royale" and "Skyfall" redefined the Bond franchise.

Lisa Marie Presley (February 1st)

The daughter of the legendary Elvis Presley, Lisa Marie Presley ventured into the music industry with her own unique style. Her debut album "To Whom It May Concern" and subsequent releases blended rock, folk, and country influences.

Guy Ritchie (September 10th)

British filmmaker Guy Ritchie made a mark with his distinct directorial style, characterized by sharp wit and unique storytelling. His early works, including "Lock, Stock and Two Smoking Barrels" and "Snatch," showcased his talent for crime comedies.

Activity: 1968 Birthdate Match-Up

Instructions: Match the notable individuals born in 1968 with their corresponding achievements or contributions. Write the letter of the accomplishment next to the correct person.

1. Will Smith	A. Co-founder of Yahoo!
2. Naomi Watts	B. Renowned for Wolverine portrayal
3. Jerry Yang	C. Hollywood icon from Philadelphia
4. Celine Dion	D. Best-selling female artist with "My Heart Will Go On"
5. Hugh Jackman	E. Notable for roles in "Mulholland Drive" and "The Ring"
6. Daniel Craig	F. Daughter of Elvis Presley, ventured into music
7. Guy Ritchie	G. Australian actor, versatile roles in film and theater
8. Lisa Marie Presley	H. ritish filmmaker known for crime comedies

Match each name with the correct letter representing their birthdate. Check your answers to see how many matches you can make!

We have heartfelt thank-you gifts for you

As a token of our appreciation for joining us on this historical journey through 1968, we've included a set of cards and stamps inspired by the year of 1968. These cards are your canvas to capture the essence of the past. We encourage you to use them as inspiration for creating your own unique cards, sharing your perspective on the historical moments we've explored in this book. Whether it's a holiday greeting or a simple hello to a loved one, these cards are your way to connect with the history we've uncovered together.

Happy creating!

Activity Answers

Chapter 1:

1. B	6. C
2. C	7. B
3. C	8. C
4. B	9. C
5. B	10. C

Chapter 2:

1. Bullitt

2. TheGraduate

3. TheOddCouple

4. HawaiiFive0

5. 60Minutes

6. Bonanza

7. Oliver

Chapter 3:

1. Hey Jude - The Beatles

2. (Sittin' On) The Dock of the Bay - Otis Redding

3. People Got to Be Free - The Rascals

4. What a Wonderful World - Louis Armstrong

5. Honey - Bobby Goldsboro

6. Those Were the Days - Mary Hopkin

7. Love is Blue - Paul Mauriat

5. "Who's sorry now? Who's sorry now?"
   - Song: "Who's Sorry Now" by Connie Francis
6. "Return to me, oh my dear, I'm so lonely"
   - Song: "Return to Me" by Dean Martin
7. "Magic moments filled with love"
   - Song: "Magic Moments" by Perry Como
8. "When the twirlin', twirlin' cavalcade of poodle skirts go by"
   - Song: "When" by The Kalin Twins

Chapter 4:

1. Billie Jean King
2. Brian Fletcher
3. AC Milan
4. Bobby Charlton
5. Jan Janssen
6. Boston Celtics beat LA Lakers (4-2)
7. George Best
8. Montreal Canadiens, J. C. Tremblay
9. Six games
10. Mickey Lolich, Tigers pitcher

Chapter 6:

1. Lamborghini
2. Jaguar
3. Alfa Romeo
4. Isuzu
5. Ginetta
6. Holden

Chapter 8:

1. C
2. E
3. A
4. D
5. G
6. B
7. H
8. F

Embracing 1968: A Grateful Farewell

Embracing 1968: A Grateful Farewell
Thank you for joining us on this journey through a year that holds a special place in our hearts. Whether you experienced 1968 firsthand or through the pages of this book, we hope it brought you moments of joy, nostalgia, and connection to a time that will forever shine brightly in our memories.

Share Your Thoughts and Help Us Preserve History

Your support and enthusiasm for this journey mean the world to us. We invite you to share your thoughts, leave a review, and keep the spirit of '68 alive. As we conclude our adventure, we look forward to more journeys through the annals of history together. Until then, farewell and thank you for the memories.
  We would like to invite you to explore more of our fantastic world by scanning the QR code below. There you can easily get free ebooks from us and receive so many surprises.

TO DO LIST

- ○ ---
- ○ ---
- ○ ---
- ○ ---
- ○ ---
- ○ ---
- ○ ---
- ○ ---
- ○ ---
- ○ ---
- ○ ---
- ○ ---
- ○ ---
- ○ ---

well done!

TO DO LIST

- ○ ------------------------------------
- ○ ------------------------------------
- ○ ------------------------------------
- ○ ------------------------------------
- ○ ------------------------------------
- ○ ------------------------------------
- ○ ------------------------------------
- ○ ------------------------------------
- ○ ------------------------------------
- ○ ------------------------------------
- ○ ------------------------------------
- ○ ------------------------------------
- ○ ------------------------------------
- ○ ------------------------------------

well done!

To Do List

- [ ] _____
- [ ] _____
- [ ] _____
- [ ] _____
- [ ] _____
- [ ] _____
- [ ] _____
- [ ] _____
- [ ] _____
- [ ] _____
- [ ] _____
- [ ] _____
- [ ] _____
- [ ] _____

To Do List

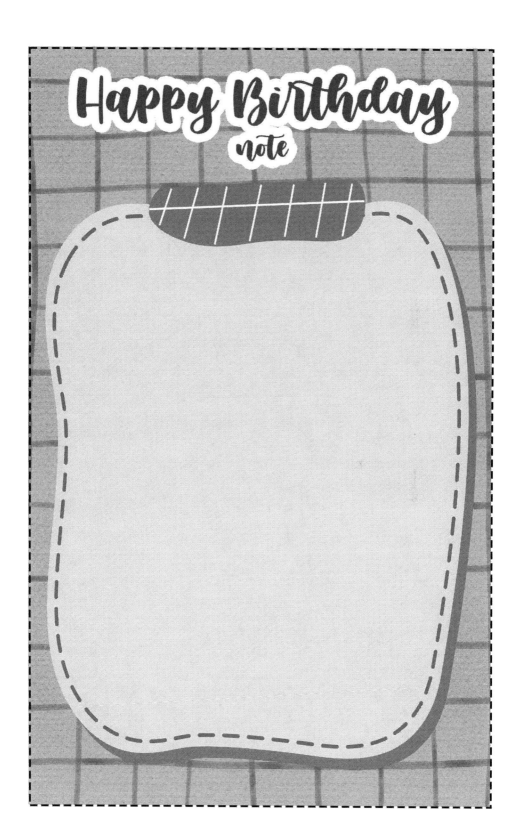

Happy Birthday
note

Happy Birthday

note

TO DO LIST

Name: _____ Day: _____ Month: _____

No	To Do List	Yes	No

TO DO LIST

Name: _____   Day: _____   Month: _____

No	To Do List	Yes	No

NOTE

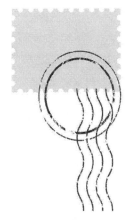

NOTE

WISH YOU WERE HERE,
123 ANYWHERE ST., ANY CITY

HAPPY BIRTHDAY NOTE

TO DO LIST

Name: _____   Day: _____   Month: _____

No	To Do List	Yes	No

NOTE

Made in the USA
Columbia, SC
16 July 2024

39bfb6d6-bcd6-42e8-a3ba-ccf8798a47f2R01